52-WEEK MOTIVATIONAL JOURNAL

52-WEEK
MOTIVATIONAL
JOURNAL

Prompts and Exercises to Inspire, Motivate, and Help You Achieve Your Goals

EMILY CASSEL

ROCKRIDGE
PRESS

Interior and Cover Designer: Lindsey Dekker
Art Producer: Meg Baggott
Editor: Crystal Nero
Production Editor: Sigi Nacson
Production Manager: Michael Kay

Cover Illustration: iStock.
Author photo courtesy of Dani McDonald

ISBN: 978-1-64876-765-4
R0

This journal is dedicated to the dream,
the vision, and the divine spark that lives
within each of us.

◇◇◇

This journal belongs to:

Emilie Dion

INTRODUCTION

Welcome to the 52-Week Motivational Journal! I'm beyond excited this journal has landed in your hands and can't wait to be your guide. Together, we'll create the necessary mindset to take action toward accelerating your growth, honing your focus, and achieving whatever goal means the most to you.

I'm Emily Cassel, an entrepreneur, Soulful Business + Leadership Coach, student of positive psychology, and lover of all things relating to personal development, growth, and spirituality. I started my own business at the age of twenty-two, so I'm no stranger to setting big, audacious goals.

There's nothing more magical, fulfilling, or powerful to me than watching someone rise to their full potential, take radical responsibility for their results, and create something incredible. While fear may arise as you begin to expand your awareness of what could be, I want to invite you to interpret that fear as evidence that the goal you're striving for is worth it. Like I tell my clients, "If the pursuit felt neutral, that would be concerning!"

For my own success, trusting in my clear vision and taking consistent steps to overcome barriers (both internal and external) has made it all possible. Whether it was launching a coaching business and attracting my soul-mate clients, healing my emotional trauma to become the most whole version of myself, manifesting and meeting the love of my life, or finding a dream home, it's all thanks to focus. And, of course, action.

What I know is this: You are here to use this one precious life in a meaningful and impactful way. What would you most love to create, achieve, or manifest in your life? It's time to get started. No more waiting, delaying, or excuses. Let's dive in, together, over the next 52 weeks.

You've got this, and I've got you.

THE MOTIVATIONAL CATALYST

I envision motivation as the fuel that keeps us energized. It propels each step toward our vision of what is possible for us to achieve, create, become, and contribute to the world around us.

That big vision, however, won't be attained all at once; rather, the ultimate greatness we desire is achieved one milestone and achievement at a time. On this 52-week journey, we'll make steady progress that builds what was once an idea, dream, or hope into reality.

When we are left to our own devices, our motivation ebbs and flows with an unpredictable cadence. When we have the self-awareness, knowledge, and tools to sustain our motivation and cultivate it consistently—rather than randomly bouncing from one extreme to the other—we make progress toward the goals we have, the results we want, and the dreams we're envisioning.

Whether your goals include shifting a behavioral pattern that's no longer serving you, mastering a new skill, becoming more creatively expressed, developing a talent or strength, or otherwise becoming the best version of yourself, you'll need to keep your motivational "fuel tank" full to follow through. The key ingredient in translating your goals from a wish to a reality is always motivation. Concerned you might not have enough? Consider this journal a great place to refill your tank. It's broken down into weeks, but feel free to reference it daily.

You may have picked up this journal because you're feeling resistant, frustrated, or defeated around a particular goal. If that's the case, then you're in the perfect place. The intention of this journal is to guide and support you in clarifying what result matters most to you to achieve. It will help you stay focused in your pursuit, help you take consistent action to build momentum, and ultimately help you achieve any goal you set.

WEEK 1

Whatever you aren't changing, you're choosing.

Before we consider what goals you want to accomplish, let's look at what's frustrating you, no longer working, or not serving you. What areas of your life feel blocked, stuck, or unfulfilling? Write down what you could improve, change, or shift to eliminate frustration, stress, and resistance to growth.

Imagine you have an identical twin who is living life free of the challenges you've just identified. What would be different about the way your identical twin experiences life, lives each day, and feels about things?

What is one action step you could take this week to begin course-correcting the areas of your life that feel out of alignment with your most fulfilling vision of what's possible?

_____

_____

_____

_____

_____

_____

Keep the Momentum ////////////////////////////////

Release Your Blocks. Grab some paper and tear it into small sections. On each piece of paper, write down the beliefs, behaviors, habits, and distractions that no longer serve you. What is holding you back from creating clarity, fulfillment, and alignment in your life? Write down everything that's taking up mental, energetic, or physical space. Schedule a few minutes this week to release them. You can tear up the pieces and recycle them or get creative with your release (like an outdoor bonfire)—as long as you do so safely!

Regardless of which method you choose, as you physically let go of what's been holding you back, imagine yourself cleansed of these old stories, habits, and drains on your time, energy, and focus.

WEEK 2

*Whether you believe you can
do a thing or not, you are right.*
—HENRY FORD

What thoughts arise in your mind when you come up with an idea, goal, or desire you wish to bring to life? Are the thoughts hopeful or doubtful?

A recurring belief is a narrative we often repeat to ourselves, without much conscious awareness, such as "I'm not smart enough to do that" or "I would do it if I had the time." List three to five recurring beliefs that block you from fully imagining what's possible or from giving yourself full permission to dream. What's the story you're telling yourself about why it's not safe, appropriate, or valuable to give yourself space to dream bigger?

What narrative would you prefer to believe that would allow you to explore an idea, dream, or goal? Cross out the negative beliefs and write empowering ones in the space below.

Keep the Momentum ////////////////////////////

Stop the Self-Sabotage. Take note of any time this week you find yourself blocking, sabotaging, or stopping yourself from considering an idea. There will be many sneaky ways these thoughts creep in! Keep a notebook with you and write them down, enter them on your phone, or write them on sticky notes. You don't need to commit fully to an idea to explore it. Allow yourself to play! Don't worry about how it will all work out. Consider what reality you would like to actively choose for yourself. Take note of what prevents you from creating it in your internal landscape.

WEEK 3

If your dreams don't scare you, they are small.
—RICHARD BRANSON

What's one goal you've considered pursuing in the past or are now considering?

Let's pretend you're going to begin pursuing that goal. What would be the scariest thing about it for you? List your fears, doubts, worries, and concerns.

What was the most surprising fear that came up for you in the previous prompt? What about that fear surprises you? Is that fear based on truth, or is it imagined?

Keep the Momentum /////////////////////////////

Future You. Close your eyes and envision yourself 20 years from today, having already achieved the kind of success you desire. Notice what your face looks like, what clothes you're wearing, what your energy feels like. What would this version of you tell you about the fears you're currently experiencing? What advice would future you offer present-day you? What would you tell yourself to stop, or start, *right now*? For five minutes each day this week, visualize your wise future self. You can ask this being for advice about anything you wish. Make note of the advice you receive.

WEEK 4

I am a powerful creator of my reality.
I am intentionally and actively choosing to see
limitless possibilities in all situations that arise.

How satisfied are you with the way your life is currently? Why?

What does your ideal day look and feel like? Paint a verbal picture of what you do, feel, and create from the time you wake up to the time you go to sleep. Make note of as many details as you can. How do you feel? What do you prioritize? What do you avoid? Be specific!

What is one new practice, habit, or shift you could make now to move closer to living your ideal day, every day of your life? Would planning out your day the night before be helpful? Meditating for 15 minutes before you get out of bed? Eliminating the word "can't" from your vocabulary this week? Pick one small change/addition.

Keep the Momentum ////////////////////////

Making the Time. Review your schedule this week. Notice where your time and attention are focused. Take note of any distractions you may be able to eliminate. Consider how much time (your most valuable nonrenewable resource) you could reclaim and direct toward a new goal each day, each week. Common excuses are that we don't have enough time, can't find the time, or are too busy to take on something new. The reality is, most of us are under-leveraging our time, energy, and attention. It's not that we don't *have* the time; it's that we aren't *making* the time.

WEEK 5

Our potential is one thing.
What we do with it is quite another.
—ANGELA DUCKWORTH

What do you know yourself to be capable of doing, being, or achieving?
What do you feel incapable of doing, being, or achieving?

Who would you be without believing you are incapable of doing, being, or achieving what you identified? What would be possible for you that currently feels impossible?

If you're being completely honest with yourself, where in your life currently do you feel you're not fully living to your full potential?

_____

_____

_____

_____

_____

_____

_____

Keep the Momentum /////////////////////////

See You for You. Have an intentional conversation with a person who knows and understands you well, and ask them the following questions: 1) What do you think I'm most naturally gifted at? 2) How would you describe my energy/presence and how I make others feel? 3) What is a big or small way I've impacted you? 4) Where do you think I could best grow, develop, or expand my potential to become my best self?

Do your best to listen without becoming too self-critical, judgmental, or attached to what comes up. Then take some time to reflect. Does their perception of you match your perception of yourself? Did any "blind spots" in your own perception of yourself pop up? Did anything about the conversation surprise you?

WEEK 6

My challenges are invitations to growth,
expansion, and new perspectives.

When you consider the goal you desire to achieve, what do you antici-
pate as the biggest hurdle or challenge you'll need to overcome?

Think back to a time when you faced a challenge and overcame it. How did you navigate and overcome the challenge? What did you learn about yourself, and how did you grow in the process?

Looking at your current goal, what would be the best possible outcome of your main challenge? Ideally, how would you go about overcoming it? What steps would you need to take? Which of your previously identified strengths and/or skills would you lean on most to navigate the challenge successfully?

Keep the Momentum ////////////////////////

Imagine Excellence. We each hold the power to write our own story and create our own narrative, so why not tell yourself an empowering one? Take a moment to close your eyes, and envision yourself successfully navigating a challenge you're presently facing in your life. Notice what your inner superhero/heroine does and doesn't do. From this new perspective of seeing yourself gliding through the situation with ease, how might you best approach this challenge moving forward?

WEEK 7

The purpose of life is not to be happy—but to matter, to be productive, to be useful, to have it make some difference that you lived at all.
—LEO ROSTEN

What qualities do you most admire and value in yourself, in others, and in the world? Why are these important to you?

If you could cultivate any new, positive feeling, characteristic, or quality to excel in, what would that be? How would that positively impact your life? How would it contribute to the pursuit of your goal?

Which qualities do you think others find least admirable in people in general, and in the world? Would you agree? Why?

Keep the Momentum /////////////////////////

Value List. Keeping our values at the forefront of our mind allows us to lead, create, and show up each day much more intentionally. For this exercise, write down the top five qualities you value most and wish to embody on a daily basis. Place this list where you'll see it each day to remind yourself and keep these values present and alive within you.

WEEK 8

I take radical responsibility, both internally
and externally, for creating the results I wish
to experience in my life.

What is the most prominent frustration you're experiencing in your
life? How does this frustration affect your ability to achieve your goal?

_____

_____

_____

_____

_____

_____

_____

_____

Let's assess the eight primary categories of your life, also known as the "Life Wheel." On a scale of 1 to 10 (1 being completely out of alignment/undesirable, 10 being completely in alignment/desirable), how would you rate your current life overall?

_____ Career   _____ Well-being

_____ Purpose   _____ Relationships

_____ Physical Environment   _____ Personal Growth

_____ Finances   _____ Play

What are the areas of your life that feel most out of alignment with your ideal vision for what's possible and your own definition of success? What are three actions you could take to increase your rating in those categories?

_____

_____

_____

_____

_____

_____

_____

_____

Keep the Momentum /////////////////////////

Life Wheel Goal Tracker. For each of the actions you determined will improve your rating in each Life Wheel category, decide which three are most important to you. Create a chart to track your follow-through on each of these actions for the next week. After taking action consistently in the targeted categories of your life, consider how different you feel. What has shifted? Would you change your rating in these three categories after this week?

WEEK 9

*The great doesn't happen through
impulse alone, and is a succession of
little things that are brought together.*
—VINCENT VAN GOGH

What is one habit, behavior, or daily ritual you would like to *stop* doing?
What would be possible for you if you stopped doing it? Why is stopping
it important to you?

When you consider your most idealized, best version of yourself, what does that version of you devote time, energy, and attention toward? What distractions does this version of you avoid?

What is one habit, behavior, or daily ritual you would like to *start* doing? What would be possible for you if you began doing this consistently? How would this new habit help you in the journey to achieve your dreams?

Keep the Momentum /////////////////////////

Stacking Up New Habits. A new habit is easier to form when it accompanies a habit that's already second nature to you, such as brushing your teeth, putting on your shoes as you walk out the door, taking a morning shower, or getting ready for bed. Choose an existing habit this week to link to your new desired habit, behavior, or daily ritual. It will be easier for you to stay consistent when it's a part of something you already do.

WEEK 10

Every day, each of us is faced with the possibility
of resetting our lives. Refocusing. Reimagining.
Rebooting. Every day, we can decide to change our
outlook, our words, our tone, our attitude.
—MARIA SHRIVER

What is one shift in perception that would allow you to expand your
view of what the pursuit of your goal could be like?

What have you been taught or conditioned to believe by the world around you about what is required of you to achieve your specific goal? List whatever comes up, without judgment around what it takes to "be successful."

If you could wave a magic wand, how would you love to feel in the process of achieving your goals or vision of success? Name three to five primary emotions you'd love to experience daily as you work toward achieving your goal. Be specific.

Keep the Momentum ////////////////////////////

Create Your Magic Wand! Since we are focusing this week on creating a more magical mindset, let's have some fun and get creative. Grab a stick from outside (or any other wandlike object) and create your own representation of a magic wand. Whenever a situation arises in which you feel frustrated, confused, or thrown off course, just pull out your magic wand and be reminded that every miracle is one shift in perception away. You get to choose your experience of any situation.

WEEK 11

*I attract, create, expect, and experience
miracles on a daily basis.*

A miracle can be a simple change in perception—an internal shift that
creates a new way of seeing what's already present in front of us, or
becoming aware of something that we were not paying attention to.
What is one miracle you would love to experience this week? What
would this change do for you right now, and how would it help move
you toward your goal?

We are often encouraged—especially after we reach a certain age or stage of life—to be "realistic" about our goals, expectations, and achievements. What are the "realistic" beliefs you are clinging to that could be distracting you from perceiving a miracle? Do you fear the vulnerability or judgment that may accompany taking a risk or straying from a more traditional, linear path?

What is in the way of your experiencing that miraculous shift right now? How might you remove that barrier and be fully open and available to receive your miracle?

Keep the Momentum ////////////////////////

Body Scan. Close your eyes and envision yourself feeling calm, centered, and present. Do a body scan of awareness from the top of your head down to your toes, inhaling and exhaling as you go, becoming increasingly aware of your internal landscape. Then envision the miracle you would love to experience this week actually happening for you. Play the situation out as if you were watching a movie in your mind. Notice any sensations—physical or emotional—that arise for you. How does it feel to receive this miracle?

WEEK 12

I am wildly capable, clear, and confident
in pursuit of what matters most to me.

Are there any aspects of your goal(s) that you are feeling unclear, confused, scattered, or uncertain about right now?

We all have insecurities that come up when we are expanding into new territory and preparing to start pursuing something worthwhile. What insecurities or doubts are arising for you now, as you further refine and clarify your goals?

What evidence have you gathered in the past that has shown, taught, or revealed to you that you are capable and wise? What past experiences can you lean on to gain confidence that can be applied to what you're currently pursuing?

Keep the Momentum /////////////////////////

Act as If. Imagine you have already achieved everything you desire for yourself at the end of 52 weeks. What would you need to be prepared for success? For example, if your goal is to buy your dream home, what are the action steps you would need to take to prepare yourself? Maybe you would begin clearing out unnecessary clutter by purging one room per week. Consider how you would shift your behavior, language, and feelings if this goal had already happened. Then take an action in alignment with this each day this week, so that you'll be prepared when the opportunity does arrive.

WEEK 13

As I bring my vision to life, I am persistent,
patient, and powerful.

Where do you notice yourself getting antsy, impatient, or frustrated in
pursuit of your goal(s)?

_____

_____

_____

_____

_____

_____

_____

_____

_____

_____

We all have nervous-system responses when we feel uncomfortable in life. Discomfort isn't always a negative experience, and the kind of discomfort that accompanies the pursuit of success or achievement isn't actually life-threatening. Unfortunately, our nervous system doesn't know the difference. How are you most likely to respond when you're working on growth and feeling uncomfortable: fight, flight, freeze, or fawn? How can you identify and accept discomfort without allowing it to turn into fear?

What happens for you—emotionally, mentally, physically—when you feel things are going too well, are too easy, or are progressing too rapidly? This, too, can trick our nervous system into feeling fear. Does this response feel most like fight, flight, freeze, or fawn?

Keep the Momentum //////////////////////////

Plan Ahead. From a centered, calm place, write a letter to yourself for when things feel challenging. What do you need to be reminded of in the moment? Consider what advice the person you most admire would give to you in that moment of peak activation. Place the letter somewhere safe so that you can pull it out and read it to yourself the next time you are feeling impatient, frustrated, or otherwise off course around your goals.

WEEK 14

I can accept failure. Everyone fails at something.
But I cannot accept not trying.
—MICHAEL JORDAN

Consider a time you thought you had "failed." How did you grow from it? Do you still consider it to be a true failure? Why or why not?

List two or three of your weaknesses. How will identifying those weaknesses make you stronger and more capable of achieving your goal? For example, will you choose a path that instead focuses on your strengths? Will you not allow the weaknesses to impede your progress? There is no wrong answer.

How can accepting your flaws make you feel stronger and more confident?

Keep the Momentum //////////////////////////

Track and Celebrate Failures. One way to measure success this week is to note how many times you take a risk and put yourself out there. In order to succeed, you have to be willing to try. Failure isn't the end of the line; it's part of the process of achieving greatness. This week, challenge yourself to take risks in relation to what you would love to achieve, and keep track of all the things that don't go according to plan. At the end of the week, feel pride in your "failures" and all the wisdom and progress you've gained by putting effort into your goal!

WEEK 15

Today is my opportunity to create the
tomorrow I want. I choose to keep going.

What is a commitment you've previously made to yourself—something
you know benefits you and supports your creating all you desire—but
have fallen off course in pursuit of recently?

It's much easier to make excuses about why we aren't where we want to be yet than to actually be honest with ourselves and take responsibility for our own results. What excuses have you made—internally or externally—about the reason you aren't yet taking action toward something that matters to you?

How will you recommit yourself this week to a commitment you've previously made and let slip? What is your plan for recommitting and making this a priority?

Keep the Momentum /////////////////////////

Find an Accountability Partner. Choose someone in your life who has the shared capacity and desire to be held accountable to achieving a result—any result. Studies show your success levels will be higher if you hold each other accountable. Your goals don't need to be the same, but they do need to be clear and measurable. Once you've clarified what you're committing to, plan to check in with each other's progress daily or weekly. You can touch base through any medium—text, e-mail, in person, phone, whatever mutually works.

WEEK 16

Discipline is built by consistently performing small acts of courage.
—ROBIN SHARMA

If you're pursuing more than one path, what is the most important goal, result, or outcome you want to achieve right now? Why does this matter to you?

Let's get *smart*! How will you objectively know whether or not you have achieved this goal? To be effective, a goal must be **S**pecific, **M**easurable, **A**ttainable, **R**ealistic, and **T**ime-oriented. Rewrite the goal you stated on the previous page so that it has these qualities.

What will be possible when you achieve this goal, create this result, or experience this particular outcome? How will your outlook, or life, change?

Keep the Momentum ///////////////////////////

Getting SMART. Now let's write the goal in an even more specific and positive way. Using a present-tense, first-person format, create an "I am" statement that expresses the feeling you'll have when you achieve your goal and why you want to achieve it. For example, if your goal is to fully transition to a plant-based diet by the end of this year, the first sentence could start with: "I am feeling energized and vibrant as I'm nourishing my body daily with a plant-based diet." This sentence is specific, and most likely attainable and realistic, but could have more detail. It also needs to be time-oriented. The second sentence could be "By the end of [date 52 weeks from your starting date], I am happily free of any foods that aren't plant-based and am surrounded by people who support my decisions/actions." You can repeat this process for goals in any area of your life that you would like to achieve.

WEEK 17

The whole point of being alive is to evolve into the
complete person you were intended to be.
—OPRAH WINFREY

If you let go of all fear of judgment from others, and if money were no
object, what would you be doing differently today?

What does living life to the fullest look and feel like for you? What does it look and feel like for you to live your most meaningful, fulfilling, and successful life? How do they differ? Be specific.

When you're not in the room, or when you're no longer living, what do you hope people say about you and the impact you've made on them?

_____

_____

_____

_____

_____

_____

_____

_____

Keep the Momentum ////////////////////////

Identify Your Success Archetypes. An archetype is a very typical example of a certain person or thing. When it comes to how you personally view and define success, who are three to five people you admire who you feel embody the qualities and characteristics you aspire to have? Compile photos of these people and write things you admire about each person below each photo. You can do this digitally or on paper. Which of those qualities do you already possess?

WEEK 18

*We cannot become what we want
by remaining what we are.*
—MAX DE PREE

Where in your life are you currently feeling too comfortable or complacent?

When we are in a holding pattern in our lives, or in a cycle of behavior that we know doesn't actually support or serve us in reaching our goals, we are gaining some form of benefit or value from the situation. We call this a "secondary gain." What do you think the secondary gain may be for you of staying in the comfort zone you identified on the previous page? Is it keeping you from a fear of failure? Are you keeping someone else happy?

Who would you be if you fully let go of that pattern of behavior or thought and allowed it to shift? What would be possible? Who could you become without that limiting you?

Keep the Momentum /////////////////////////

Push Your Growth Edge. Find one small way to get uncomfortable this week. It could be as simple and small as changing your approach to something you do daily, like brushing your teeth with your non-dominant hand. It could be something bigger, like learning a new language or skill. Whatever form of constructive discomfort you decide to commit to, be consistent and track your progress. As you practice normalizing discomfort, notice and reflect on how much more capable you are of pushing your growth edges simply by allowing yourself to feel uncomfortable.

WEEK 19

I am brave, bold, and audacious with my dreams. I am worthy of receiving all my desires.

Where do you believe your worth originates? What makes you deserving of the success you desire?

_____

_____

_____

_____

_____

_____

_____

_____

_____

_____

Most of us have been conditioned to believe that we have to earn worthiness and that whether we are deserving of the results or experiences we want is contingent on certain factors or actions. What have you learned are the contingencies to your success/happiness/fulfillment? List them. Are they telling the truth? Spoiler alert: You don't *earn* worthiness. It's already yours!

What would you love to believe about your inherent worthiness that would better support you in feeling deserving of all the goodness you desire? What inner dialogue do you need to change to accept your worthiness?

_____

_____

_____

_____

_____

_____

_____

Keep the Momentum /////////////////////////

Reconnect with Your Inner Child. Find a photo of yourself as a child. If you don't have one handy, call to mind an image of yourself as a child. What would you tell this sweet, innocent being about their worthiness? Say (out loud or internally) to your inner child: "Your worth is inherent. There's nothing you can ever do or not do to change that. You are deserving because you are alive." If it feels supportive, place this photo somewhere you can see it often, to reconnect with your inherent worthiness and remember these truths. When your mind wants to try to convince you otherwise, override it.

WEEK 20

The key is not to prioritize what's on your schedule,
but to schedule your priorities.
—STEPHEN COVEY

What stops you from taking consistent action toward what you want to achieve?

_____

_____

_____

_____

_____

_____

_____

_____

Distractions in our environment—whether they're other people, competing tasks or responsibilities, technology, or anything that seems urgent or important to us in a given moment—are a normal part of life. What or who pulls your attention to something else and distracts you from spending the necessary time on goal-oriented activities throughout the week?

What one distraction can you commit to eliminating this week? How will you ensure it's eliminated?

Keep the Momentum /////////////////////////

Do the Most Important Things First. This week, identify the most important task or action item for each day. Then carve out time to complete it first, before the many distractions of the day enter your awareness or affect your progress. You may need to turn off notifications, put your phone on airplane mode, and/or alert those around you that you'll be unavailable for a certain period of time. You may find this so helpful it turns into a standard habit!

WEEK 21

*I find joy in the small moments. I notice
beauty in the mundane.*

What is one action, habit, or thought that can instantly improve your
mood? Does it make you smile, energize you, bring a sense of calm?
How can it be useful in your journey to achieve your goal?

What is one moment in your life you are deeply grateful for? Why are you so grateful for this moment, above all others?

What experience that gave you a sense of overwhelming awe and wonder would you choose to repeat over and over again?

_____

_____

_____

_____

_____

_____

_____

Keep the Momentum ///////////////////////////

Go on an Appreciation Adventure. Spend some time this week unplugged from technology, and go somewhere that you consider to be beautiful. You may choose a place that's familiar and that you visit often, or a brand-new place you've never been to but have always wished to go to. Spend at least an hour in this place, with the intention of finding as many things to appreciate as you can. Notice the sounds, sights, and situations you encounter. Find something to be grateful for about each of them. Remember that the feeling of gratitude and a sense of awe are always available to you. We often direct our attention to the things that bother us. You can always choose to refocus!

WEEK 22

In the middle of difficulty lies opportunity.
—ALBERT EINSTEIN

As you consider your main goal, think of someone you feel might be standing in your way or has prevented you from achieving success in the past. Do (or did) they really hold the power to stop you?

The combination of intentional action and taking a chance is powerful. It doesn't always pay off the way we hope it will, but nothing truly great happens without the combination of effort and taking a chance. What risk can you take this week to contribute to moving forward toward your goal?

What's the best thing that could happen when you take that risk?

Keep the Momentum /////////////////////////////

Have a Courageous Conversation. This week, I invite you to venture into the territory of vulnerability, which can feel scary and difficult for most of us. The beautiful thing about vulnerability is that it opens up space for us to experience deeper levels of joy, creativity, innovation, intimacy, depth, and pretty much all the positive emotions and experiences we desire more of! Who is someone with whom you currently hold tension, in a relationship of any kind, that you would like to alleviate? Initiate a conversation with this person and approach it with love, compassion, respect, and understanding. Be willing to listen. Be open to really hearing the other person. Enjoy setting both of you free from the tension.

WEEK 23

I will focus on the one step in front of me,
not the whole staircase that lies ahead.

Where are you "getting ahead of yourself" and worrying too much
about the bigger picture, instead of focusing on the step directly in
front of you?

_____

_____

_____

_____

_____

_____

_____

_____

_____

Fear of failure prevents many people from taking the necessary action to reach their goals. What most people call "failure" is really just a shortsighted assessment of something that didn't meet their expectations about what they *thought* would happen, or their own judgment of what they thought *should* have happened. Failure, then, is often a narrow and limited view of life unfolding exactly as it's meant to, to teach us the lessons we'll need to apply later. True "failure" happens only when we give up and stop trying. If you never quit, you'll never fail—and you'll always win. What are you committed to never giving up on?

What is the immediate next step you need to take in order to make progress toward bringing your vision to life?

Keep the Momentum /////////////////////////////

Map Out Your Action Steps. Set up a project management system using free software, like Asana or Trello, and "brain-dump" all the tasks needed to happen to get you from point A (where you are currently) to point Z (your desired result). Assign each task to yourself with a reasonable due date. Build upon the completion of a previous task to stay accountable to following through. It's so much easier and feels more manageable to achieve something when we are clear on the exact steps to get there. Think of it as creating a recipe for your success. You have to know the ingredients and follow clear directions in order to bake your success cake!

WEEK 24

Be curious, ask questions, build things and ignore the notion of boundaries. You'll be surprised to see how many people will want to join you for the ride and help you along the way.

—CAROLINE PUGH

When working on a challenging project, what one thing do you say to yourself most often? Are you your own cheerleader, or are you more prone to negative self-talk?

Many people believe that the only way to change is to be harsh, critical, or judgmental to ourselves. Good news: This is not the case! We get so much farther, so much faster, when we choose curiosity over self-criticism. Where are you being unkind to yourself about your progress toward achieving your goals?

How can you rework those negative thoughts into helpful encourage-ments? What's an empowering question to ask yourself, or statement to tell yourself, that would be based in curiosity and self-compassion instead of judgment and self-blame?

Keep the Momentum /////////////////////////

Identify Your Conditions for Thriving. Make a list of the top five things that create the proper conditions for you to feel inspired, clear, confident, and focused. How can you help bring peak/optimal performance to all that you do this week? Here are some things you might consider including: 5 minutes of mindful med-itation, moving your body for at least 20 minutes, listening to an inspiring podcast, consuming (or avoiding) certain foods, having a solo dance party to a favorite song, or connecting with a loved one. Let this be personal to you.

WEEK 25

The only happiness I can control is my own. I take full
responsibility for creating and cultivating my own joy
daily, regardless of the circumstances life presents.

How do you want to feel as you achieve your goals? List five emotions
that represent how you would feel if you were living in alignment with
your highest potential.

Often, the way we expect to feel once we achieve a long-term goal is already available to us in the present moment. There is no reason to wait. How do you think you will feel once you achieve the goal you're working toward?

What's one habit, practice, or behavior you could implement now in order to cultivate those feelings in the present moment and in the process of pursuing your goal?

Keep the Momentum ///////////////////////////

Create Your Emotional Vision Board. Find a photo of yourself where you are fully alive and fulfilled. If you don't have a photo that feels this way to you, use any image you feel accurately represents the state of being you desire. Now write the five most desired feelings you've identified this week and overlay the list of desired feelings on the photo either digitally or by hand. Display this image where you'll see and be able to connect to it daily. Use it as a visual reminder that you hold the power to feel the way you want to feel in every moment of your day.

WEEK 26

I am resilient. I am powerful. I am resourceful.

Where do you feel most powerful in your life? Why?

It's easy for us to fall into the trap of giving our power away or out-sourcing our decisions to circumstances, people, and situations beyond ourselves—and therefore, outside our control. List three to five ways you tend to give your power away.

What is one way you can reclaim that power you've previously given away to something or someone outside yourself?

_____

_____

_____

_____

_____

_____

_____

Keep the Momentum //////////////////////////

Call All Your Power Back to You. Close your eyes, and focus on your breath. Begin to notice any thoughts, energy, or awareness that is lingering in other places, in other times (past or future), or with other people. Envision each of these as a cord of light or energy that represents your power, which you can reel back in as if you were reeling in a fishing line. As you reel each cord of energy back in, say silently or aloud, "I take my power back from anywhere and everywhere I have given it away, consciously or unconsciously, now." You can envision reeling each power cord back into your heart, or any place in your physical body that feels intuitively right for you. Repeat this process as many times as needed to feel your power restored and fully reclaimed.

WEEK 27

*We delight in the beauty of a butterfly
but rarely admit the changes it has
gone through to achieve that beauty.*
—MAYA ANGELOU

How does overemphasizing the gap between you and your goal affect
your progress?

We get in life what we're willing to tolerate. Where and what are you "tolerating" in your life right now, instead of changing or fixing? How is this affecting your progress toward achieving your goal(s)?

What is the most constructive thing to focus on this week, to make consistent progress toward your goal(s)?

_____

_____

_____

_____

_____

_____

_____

Keep the Momentum ////////////////////////////

Define Your Weekly Nonnegotiables. Most people fail to achieve greatness because they get stuck oscillating between two extremes: first, doing everything they can to achieve something, which burns them out, and then taking on a period of inaction, which makes no progress toward their goals. They end up right back where they started, with no net gain. Sound familiar? Make a list of small, steady action steps you can take to maintain a sustainable pace of weekly progress toward achieving your goals. Schedule these actions, habits, rituals, or activities in your calendar. Set reminders to make follow-through as simple as possible.

WEEK 28

If we have our own why in life,
we shall get along with almost any how.
—NIETZSCHE, AS TRANSLATED BY VIKTOR FRANKL

Why are the goals you're currently pursuing meaningful to you? Are they in line with your life's purpose?

_____

_____

_____

_____

_____

_____

_____

_____

_____

As human beings, our motivations are rooted in avoiding pain and maximizing pleasure. In the midst of pursuing your current goal, what is the pain you are attempting to avoid? What is the pleasure you are moving toward? Is either at the expense of another person?

What would shift in your life, and in the lives of those around you, as a result of avoiding this pain and maximizing this pleasure?

Keep the Momentum ////////////////////////

Write a Personal Mission Statement. A personal mission statement will help you remember why you're doing what you're doing each day, and why the discomfort you'll face in pursuit of your goal is worthwhile. Without being clear on our *why*, we become overly focused on the *how* of any situation. We can easily talk ourselves out of taking the necessary action that would create meaningful change in our lives and in the world. A personal mission statement answers the question "Why are you here on this planet, and what are you here to contribute?" Here is an example of Oprah Winfrey's personal mission statement: "To be a teacher. And to be known for inspiring my students to be more than they thought they could be." Once you've written your personal mission statement, frame it and display it somewhere you'll see daily.

WEEK 29

You can't go back and make a new start, but you can start right now and make a brand new ending.
—JAMES SHERMAN

Where do you derive your strength from during times when you feel challenged, tested, or pushed to your limits?

We all go through challenging times, and the darkness that accompanies those hardships can both scare us and strengthen us. What has been the hardest or scariest thing you've ever had to face in your life so far? How did you handle it?

What have you learned about yourself, and the source of your own strength, through facing this challenging time?

_____

_____

_____

_____

_____

_____

_____

_____

Keep the Momentum ///////////////////////////

Choose Your Power Pose or Power Move. Our body language and posture can influence our brain and body chemistry. Research suggests that selecting a more "expansive" posture, such as your hands on your hips, chest broad, chin lifted, will help you feel more confident. Choose a posture or a "move" to link to a certain behavior or emotional state. If you want to overcome nerves before an important meeting, for example, come up with a power move to do immediately prior. Strike your personal power pose!

WEEK 30

I am showing up fully to create the outcome I desire.
I cast my reasons aside, in favor of results.

What has been one of the most powerful decisions you've made in
your life so far? How has this decision shaped your life path?

Our decision not to make a choice is the decision to stay exactly where we are and not move forward. Where are you currently being indecisive, and therefore unwilling to choose progress?

What has been a moment in your life when you acted indecisively? What was the outcome of the decision not to make a clear choice?

Keep the Momentum ///////////////////////

Practice Being Decisive. Get comfortable with making gut-instinct decisions and choices, and then accepting them. No second-guessing yourself or having FOMO (**F**ear **O**f **M**issing **O**ut). Observe what your "yes" feels like and what your "no" feels like—emotionally, physically, and mentally. Notice how you feel when you've made a decision that you regret, versus one that you feel great about. Practice being decisive with little decisions this week—like what to eat for dinner or what clothes you'll wear for the day—to get confident making larger ones.

WEEK 31

*Playing big is being more loyal
to your dreams than your fears.*
—TARA MOHR

What would playing big in your life and in your pursuit of your goals look and feel like to you? In other words, if you were choosing to act from your desires, rather than your fears, what would change?

_____

_____

_____

_____

_____

_____

_____

_____

_____

Where are you currently playing small in your life? In other words, where are you holding back from putting yourself out there, for fear of being rejected, being criticized, or not belonging?

What is one action you will take this week to play bigger and create more opportunity for yourself?

_____

_____

_____

_____

_____

_____

_____

Keep the Momentum /////////////////////////

Set a Date for Your Next Leap. When preparing to take a leap, we can feel scared. Resistance and fear might bubble up inside us, which creates hesitancy. We may begin to doubt or question ourselves or convince ourselves we don't need to actually take action. Setting a date and putting it in the calendar can help us avoid getting derailed. This week, pick one thing you're feeling most resistant to, set a date for it on your calendar, and make it a nonnegotiable, done deal. No loopholes allowed! Get excited, because it's happening!

WEEK 32

I gather evidence daily that I am making progress
and bringing my vision to life. I celebrate my small
victories along the journey.

How could you celebrate your small victories and wins along the journey toward a bigger achievement?

We are often our own worst critic when it comes to achieving our goals and making progress toward them. What is the story you're telling yourself when you fall short of achieving what you set out to achieve or don't follow through? What does your internal dialogue sound like?

What is one uplifting reminder you can give yourself the next time you're feeling unmotivated in pursuit of your goal and want to keep going? What would your inner mentor (instead of your inner critic) tell you?

Keep the Momentum ///////////////////////

Amplify Your Little Victories. Each day this week, find something small to celebrate. It can be that you meditated for 5 minutes, had the most delicious cup of coffee, or made a tiny amount of progress toward your goal. Whatever the small win, talk about it (to yourself or to someone else) as though it is the greatest thing that's ever happened in your life! Get specific and detailed about all the things that are amazing about it—the things you loved about the experience, how grateful you are, how excited you are that it happened. Celebrate it as though you have just won the lottery or achieved the big goal you're pursuing! Feel that sense of celebration. Get into the habit of celebrating small victories along the way.

WEEK 33

*Failure is only the opportunity to
more intelligently begin again.*
—HENRY FORD

What scares you most about not achieving your goals or being
successful?

The road to success is paved with multiple failures. The question is not whether you will fail; it's how you will pick yourself up again when you inevitably do fail. Doing what it takes to succeed in any goal will involve uncertainty, growth, and vulnerability. How will you pick yourself back up when you fall so that you can apply what you've learned throughout the process? How will you show you've grown as a result?

What word could you use to replace the word "failure" when you talk about achieving your goal? Choose something that feels more neutral or empowering.

Keep the Momentum ////////////////////////////

Write a Personal Success Manifesto. Your personal manifesto should be uplifting, use strong and clear language, and be written in the first person and present tense, with positive words (for example, "I am courageous" instead of "I will not be afraid"). It can be as short or as long as you'd like. The intention behind your personal manifesto is to compile a list of empowering and motivating affirmations that represent what you most value, why achieving your goals is important to you, and how you define success on your own terms.

WEEK 34

Hope is a form of planning.
—GLORIA STEINEM

Where are you currently being more loyal to your fears than your hopes?

Try to consider fear on this journey as **F**alse **E**vidence **A**ppearing **R**eal. What scares you the most about pursuing the goals you've set for yourself?

Often, we aren't seeing wanted results because of misalignments in our beliefs about what's possible, the action we're taking, and the words we affirm to ourselves. How might you shift your actions, beliefs, and words to align more fully with your hopes than your fears? What would you need to believe, do, or speak aloud to yourself or others to create the results you want?

Keep the Momentum /////////////////////////

Overcome Your F.E.A.R. Many of our modern-day fears have little to do with our own survival; instead of being protective and helpful, they become limitations to our success. We see false realities that we convince ourselves are true. Identify your top three fears that block you from experiencing your peak fulfillment and success. For each fear, identify what evidence you have that it is valid. Now break down that fear. For example, a fear of public speaking might prevent you from becoming a teacher. What is that fear based on? What do you think will happen if you speak in public? How can you view that fear in a new, less scary light?

WEEK 35

Everything I go through is preparing me
to receive what I've asked for.
I am always evolving and growing.

What is feeling overwhelming, frustrating, or uncertain for you
this week?

Feeling overwhelmed can come from a belief that we don't already have the resources, tools, or capacity within us to create what we desire in any given situation. In the situations that are currently feeling overwhelming for you, what is it specifically that you feel you are lacking?

How do you want to feel instead of overwhelmed, frustrated, or uncertain? List three emotions you would rather feel, and include one action you could take this week to cultivate these preferred emotional states.

Keep the Momentum ////////////////////////

Swap "Have to" for "Get to." The words we use to describe our life experience are powerful, and they determine how we perceive and filter every situation we face. This week, try to replace the phrase "have to" with "get to" in your daily conversations. Notice how this shifts your energy. Challenge yourself to write down three phrases in which you'll replace "I have to" with "I get to" this week. Notice how this small shift allows you to feel more excited and open, versus frustrated and shut down.

WEEK 36

What specific tasks or action items feel particularly challenging for you this week? How are they interrupting your goal?

Pleasure is a highly productive state of being, because it's energized and expansive. How can you infuse more pleasure into the tasks that feel challenging for you this week? How can you make the task at hand more fun or enjoyable for yourself so that you're approaching it from a place of flow, not a place of force?

What are the activities, people, and experiences that cultivate the most pleasure in your life? How can they support you in achieving your goal?

Keep the Momentum ///////////////////////

Make Your Pleasure List. On a sheet of paper or in a note on your phone, make a list of all the free activities that bring you pleasure. Make another list of all the pleasure-evoking activities that cost money. Challenge yourself to add at least five activities to each list! Keep this list handy. Refer back to it whenever you need a jolt of pleasure or a shift in your state of mind.

WEEK 37

I didn't come this far just to come this far.
My consistency is paying off in ways big
and small, seen and yet to be seen.

What are you most proud of yourself for accomplishing, creating, or becoming in pursuit of your goals?

_____

_____

_____

_____

_____

_____

_____

_____

_____

_____

Pretend you are hearing the story of your progress toward your goals from an outside perspective. What positive things could someone listening to the story of your journey thus far say about you?

If you keep showing up the way you have been recently, will your vision come to life? Why or why not?

Keep the Momentum ///////////////////////

Track Your Consistency (Not Your Results). This week, decide on one simple thing you can do consistently that, if done repeatedly, will add up to a larger result and support your long-term goals. Track this behavior, habit, or action. By the end of the week, how do you feel having taken consistent action and allowed it to be simple?

WEEK 38

The two most important days in life are the day you
were born and the day you discover why.
—ANONYMOUS

What sets your soul on fire? What gets you fired up, energized, and
excited to take action?

We all hold different definitions and unique formulas for what creates happiness in our lives. What are the things you fill your life with that bring the most happiness and satisfaction?

What would you do with your life if you had guaranteed success? What would you pursue or do differently if you were strictly motivated by what brought you happiness?

Keep the Momentum /////////////////////////////

Make Yourself a Happy Playlist. Music has the power to anchor us to an emotional state quickly. Take time this week to create a playlist of your favorite songs, ones that make you feel truly happy. Listen to this playlist whenever you need to lift your spirits. Throw yourself a solo dance party, take a car ride, or share the soundtrack at your next gathering with loved ones!

WEEK 39

*Never give up on a dream just because
of the time it will take to accomplish it.
The time will pass anyway.*
—EARL NIGHTINGALE

Pursuing a new goal has its good moments and bad moments. Have
you fallen off track while pursuing your intended goal at any point in
this journey?

One of the biggest excuses people make about why they haven't accomplished a goal or followed through on something important is that they don't have enough time. Where are you making this excuse currently in your life? How is it impacting your progress?

What do you need to recommit to this week in order to feel back on track?

_____

_____

_____

_____

_____

_____

_____

Keep the Momentum ////////////////////////

Create a State of Time Abundance. Our mindset can be either our greatest ally or our worst enemy when it comes to pursuing our goals. This week, be on the lookout for where you're telling yourself a limiting story about how much time you have or don't have. Any time you catch yourself in a belief about not having enough time, instead choose to replace it with the affirmation "I always have enough time." See how this energetically flips the script and allows you to stretch, expand, and bend time to your will; time will work with you instead of against you.

WEEK 40

My mind is full of brilliant ideas
and creative solutions.

What inspires you to keep going when things feel challenging?

Reflect back on a time when you felt things were out of sorts, chaotic, or not working in your favor. In hindsight, how would your present-day perspective help that past, worried version of yourself feel reassured?

What evidence are you receiving that shows what you have been working toward is on its way to you?

_____

_____

_____

_____

_____

_____

_____

_____

Keep the Momentum /////////////////////////

Brain-Dump Your Brilliance. You can focus this exercise around a specific problem or challenge that you're facing, or a desire you have that feels distant. List as many potential solutions or opportunities as possible, without thinking too much about the feasibility of each or worrying about being realistic. Just put your pen to paper and let the ideas flow. Set a timer for 10 minutes and don't stop writing until the timer goes off. Look back at your list when you're finished and highlight or circle a few of the best ideas you came up with, then put them into action!

WEEK 41

Be happy with what you have while working for what you want.
—HELEN KELLER

What are three things you're grateful for this week? Why do you appreciate each?

Looking at the list of three things you're grateful for, do you think you'll have the same level of appreciation for those three things once you've achieved your main goal? Why or why not?

How, where, and to whom can you express more gratitude for the positive aspects of your journey?

Keep the Momentum ///////////////////////////

The Gratitude 10. Make a list of 10 things you're grateful for. They can be simple or complex, big or small, human or inanimate. Now challenge yourself to search for and write down 10 more things to be grateful for in your life, both inside yourself (a beating heart, breath in your lungs, your eyesight, etc.) and outside yourself (loved ones, your favorite food, a beautiful sunset, etc.). Whenever you're feeling defeated or out of sorts, revisit this list and remind yourself of all there is to be grateful for right now.

WEEK 42

I put my energy into what matters most to me.
I am becoming closer to my highest and
best self each day.

How do you define success internally and externally in your life?

Recall a situation in which you were spending your energy, focus, and attention on things that did not support your goals, dreams, or desires. What was the outcome of the situation? What did you learn about yourself from the experience?

What do you need to trust, surrender, and/or accept this week to allow progress to flow more freely?

Keep the Momentum /////////////////////////

Clear the Clutter. Clear the mental, physical, and emotional clutter in your life. Our physical environment matters when it comes to being able to stay focused. Take note this week of where in your physical environment things have become cluttered, excessive, or disorganized. Pick one room or area. Carve out a few hours to sort through the clutter and eliminate it from your energetic field. Release the things that no longer serve you by responsibly discarding, donating, recycling, or selling them. Take a deep breath of release. Look at the freed space. Doesn't that feel so much better?!

WEEK 43

I am willing to boldly face any storm that
comes my way, knowing that the discomfort and
change it brings is temporary.

What's a storm you've faced—currently or in the recent past—on the
path of pursuing your goals?

The only certainty in life is uncertainty. What uncertainties have you faced, or do you expect to face, in pursuit of your goals?

How can you approach the uncertainties inherent in your path toward your highest potential?

Keep the Momentum /////////////////////////

Delegate to the Universe. This week, whenever something arises that is out of your control that you're tempted to become sucked into, distracted by, or overly worried about, write it down. Anything that causes tension in your body, mind, or emotions this week, write it on this to-do list for the Universe, and know it is being taken care of. It could be something tangible, like "Clean the bathroom" when you don't want to do it, or as intangible as "Forgive my friend." Notice how your energy and focus can shift away from those tasks and back into what's within your control. You may even receive little hits of inspiration or energy, or experience the synchronicity of things just working themselves out without your having to lift a finger!

WEEK 44

My direction is more important than my speed.
I am focused on aligning my actions with
my vision each day.

Where in your life do you get frustrated by things taking longer than
you want them to, or longer than expected?

What happens when you become impatient? How does your impatience create a ripple effect in your life and experience? Is it constructive or destructive? Why?

How might you practice more patience with yourself, others, and your goals? How are presence and patience connected?

_____

_____

_____

_____

_____

_____

_____

_____

Keep the Momentum ////////////////////////////

Let Go of Shoulds. Impatience can be a result of thinking something should have happened by now. Yet *should be* has no effect or impact on what *is*. This week, if you find yourself getting impatient because you think something should be something that it isn't, stop yourself. Your expectation changes nothing. Accept what is (or isn't) in front of you to release yourself from the power of "should."

WEEK 45

We should all have the absolute and inalienable right to define ourselves.

—CHELSEA MANNING

Where do you take things too personally or overvalue the opinions, words, or actions of others?

_____

_____

_____

_____

_____

_____

_____

_____

_____

Nothing other people do (or don't do) is because of you; rather, it is because of their own perceptions, their conditioning, and the reality they live in, inside their own minds. What assumptions do you make about other people's behavior toward you?

What's the story you create and tell yourself in your own mind about what other people's behaviors, actions, or emotions mean about you?

Keep the Momentum /////////////////////////

Do "the Work." Byron Katie created a four-question process of self-inquiry called "the Work." It is quite simple and involves asking yourself four questions about any belief that causes pain. The questions are: 1) Is it true? 2) Can you absolutely know that it's true? 3) How do you react when you believe that thought? 4) Who would you be without the thought? This week, select one of the assumptions or stories you've identified above and run it through these four questions. You'll find it frees you from being internally bound by negative thoughts.

WEEK 46

I choose to see rejection as redirection. When I am
tired, I rest instead of quitting or giving up.

While working toward your goal, where have you faced rejection, from
either another person or a situation, that made you feel like your path
forward was blocked?

Progress toward any goal cannot be too extreme or intense for a sustained period; otherwise we will easily burn out, give up, or start building resentment toward the goal. What helps you create a more sustainable pace or rhythm of working toward a big goal over a prolonged period of time? For example, a sustainable middle-ground step toward going 100 percent plant-based that you can take in the next week, when you're currently eating a meat-and-dairy-heavy diet, might be to buy 50 percent fewer animal products and 50 percent more vegetables than you typically would. Attempting to go 100 percent from the start is bound to cause enough frustration to warrant quitting.

What have you been taught, told, or conditioned to believe about resting, taking breaks, or slowing down? What are the limiting beliefs, stories, or narratives playing out in your mind around these themes?

Keep the Momentum /////////////////////////

Make Space to Rest. Consider the activities, rituals, and behaviors that bring you the most restoration. What can you do to return to your work feeling more energized, clear, and focused? Build in some time each day for smaller increments of rest. At least once a week, build in longer periods of restful activities. Schedule them into your calendar as if they are important appointments. Set reminders so that it's easy to follow through.

WEEK 47

*I am grateful for all the unknowns and
uncertainties of my past, present, and future.
I choose to see growth, opportunity, and
adventure in every unknown on my path.*

What do you now know about pursuing the goals you set that you were
unaware of or blind to when you decided to pursue them?

When we set our sights on a new goal, what we don't know can actually protect us from crippling fear and being overwhelmed. What are the things that, had you known they would happen, might have stopped you from ever getting started?

If you could go back in time and tell yourself anything about setting and pursuing the goals you chose, what would you advise your previous self to do or not do?

_____

_____

_____

_____

_____

_____

_____

_____

Keep the Momentum ////////////////////////////

Look Forward by Looking Back. Write a letter to your past self, the person you were at the beginning of this journey. What advice or encouragement would you give to yourself, knowing what you now know? Consider the kinds of things you might say to a friend, loved one, mentee, or younger sibling to prepare them for a worthwhile, albeit uncertain, journey ahead.

WEEK 48

Each day, I become stronger, wiser, and more capable of creating the reality I desire. Through steady progress forward, I can be the architect of any dream I can envision for myself and the world.

What processes have you implemented in the pursuit of your goals that have supported you in staying steady, focused, and consistent?

Looking at your overall life journey—not just the one toward your goal—what percentage of your success do you attribute to hard work? What percentage do you attribute to luck? Why did you choose this distribution of credit?

What three situations have shown you how capable you are of achieving what you set out to accomplish?

Keep the Momentum /////////////////////////

Sort Luck from Hard Work. Luck is where opportunity meets preparation. What role did your hard work actually play in any perceived luck that you've experienced in the pursuit of your goal? Give yourself credit for allowing that luck to happen.

WEEK 49

Be passionate and be involved in what you believe in. And do it as thoroughly and honestly and fearlessly as you can.
—ROSEMARIE COLVIN, COMMENTING ON MARIE COLVIN'S LEGACY

What matters most to you? What do you most value in yourself, others, and the world around you?

When we're honest with ourselves, true transformation can occur. What has been the most powerful transformation or breakthrough you've experienced in pursuit of your goals?

What fears have you overcome throughout the process of pursuing your goals? Which are you most proud of overcoming?

Keep the Momentum ////////////////////////

What's Your Legacy? It may sound a bit morbid, but this week, let's consider your own metaphorical obituary. What do you hope to have accomplished? How do you hope to be remembered after your time here on Earth is complete? List your desired accomplishments, hobbies, moments, meaningful relationships, and anything else that feels relevant to your impact over the course of your lifetime.

WEEK 50

I am the artist of my own life. My life is a blank
canvas, and I am creating a masterpiece.

What is one thing you've committed to in the past that you have not followed through on? How do you feel about the lack of follow-through?

You always reserve the right to change your mind. However, it's also important to retain integrity and follow through on your word. Consider a situation in which a change of mind did not align with your external commitment. How did you proceed or handle the situation?

Is there anything you have let slide and not followed through on but feel is important to your growth and progress? Is this something you want to recommit to or release permanently?

Keep the Momentum ////////////////////////////

Make a "No" List. List everything you wish you could say no to. The list can be as long or as brief as you'd like. Then choose one thing, circle it, and start saying no to that thing this week, gracefully and with love. Notice what shifts as a result. The more we say no to what's out of alignment for us, the more space we make for opportunities that are a yes.

WEEK 51

*What lies behind us and what lies before
us are small matters compared to what lies within
us. And when we bring what is within us out into
the world, miracles happen.*
—STANLEY HASKINS

What new skills or attributes have you acquired this past year in the
process of setting and pursuing your goals?

_____

_____

_____

_____

_____

_____

_____

Who have you become in the process of pursuing your goals? Who have you un-become? Use the prompt "I have become/un-become someone who . . ." and write down as many specific observations as you can.

What has been your biggest challenge? Your biggest win?

Keep the Momentum /////////////////////////

List Your Achievements. Flip back through your calendar, the pages of this journal, and any other tools you've used to track your progress throughout the past 51 weeks. Take note of the most significant milestones and wins, both big and small. List everything you can, even (and especially) if it feels too small to write down. Take note of how achieving each item on your list created a ripple effect in other areas of your life, too. Make note of those shifts, changes, and growth points. You can continue adding to your list as more memories come back to you throughout this week. Once your list feels complete, read it out loud to yourself or a loved one so that it feels more real. Celebrate how far you've come and how much you've grown!

WEEK 52

I honor the challenges, the lessons, and the
barriers that have taught me how to be resilient and
persevere through anything that arises on my path
toward internal and external successes. There is so
much more for me to accomplish in this world and
in my lifetime. I am ready, excited, and willing to see
the limitless possibilities revealed to me now.

Looking back on your journey over the last 52 weeks, what one thing
are you most proud of? What are you most grateful for?

Did you achieve the goals you set for yourself 52 weeks ago? Why or why not? Looking back, is there anything you would have done differently?

What's one practice, habit, or behavior that was unfamiliar to you at the beginning of your pursuit but now feels like a nonnegotiable part of your day?

Keep the Momentum /////////////////////////

Envision Your Next Level. The cycle of becoming the best version of yourself, contributing to the world around you by using your gifts and talents, and creating an impact is never-ending! Take some space this week to journal about what your next-level self and next-level life will look and feel like. From a perspective of limitless possibility, what would you most love to achieve, create, accomplish, or contribute moving forward? You can do it!

RESOURCES

AuthenticHappiness.org—The University of Pennsylvania's hub for exploring positive psychology through helpful resources, trainings, books, and questionnaires to support living a more fulfilling life.

***The Big Leap: Conquer Your Hidden Fear and Take Life to the Next Level* by Gay Hendricks**—*New York Times* bestseller on learning how to overcome our single barrier to happiness, fulfillment, and success in all areas of life.

EmilyCassel.com/free—A curated library of free tools, resources, and trainings to help you take a business idea to launch, grow or scale an existing business, and activate your soul's mission.

***Grit: The Power of Passion and Perseverance* by Angela Duckworth**—This is truly a must-read if you have a tendency to compare yourself to others, doubt your own abilities or talents, and/or are inconsistent in trying to reach your goals.

Insight Timer app—An excellent free library of searchable, easy-to-follow guided meditations to navigate the clarification, pursuit, and achievement of any goal. The app is easy to use and will always be in your pocket when you need it!

***Unlocking Us* podcast with Brené Brown**—A compilation of stories of brave and brokenhearted moments that will inspire almost anyone. Listen at brenebrown.com/podcast/introducing-unlocking-us.

VIACharacter.org—Take the free VIA Survey of Character Strengths to learn about your best qualities and learn how to leverage your strengths in all you do, from the VIA Institute on Character.

The Work of Byron Katie—Visit TheWork.com for free downloadable worksheets and further information about how to free yourself from the thoughts that cause suffering.

REFERENCES

ABC 30. "Maya Angelou Quotes." ABC 30 Action News, April 4, 2019. abc30.com/maya-angelou-quotes-and-still-i-rise-in-someone -elses-cloud/81643.

Beaumont, Peter. "Marie Colvin Experienced War Alongside Those Who Suffered in War." *Guardian*, February 22, 2012.

BrainyQuote. "Aristotle Quotes." Accessed February 20, 2021. brainyquote.com/quotes/aristotle_377765.

———. "Max De Pree Quotes." BrainyQuote.com. Accessed February 5, 2021. brainyquote.com/quotes/max_de_pree_377124.

———. "Stephen Covey Quotes." BrainyQuote.com. Accessed April 8, 2021. brainyquote.com/quotes/stephen_covey_133504.

Duckworth, Angela. *Grit: The Power of Passion and Perseverance.* Simon and Schuster, 2016.

Ford, Henry, with Samuel Crowther. *My Life and Work.* Doubleday, Page & Company, 1923.

Frankl, Viktor. *Man's Search for Meaning.* Beacon Press, 1959.

Goodreads. "Albert Einstein Quotes." Goodreads.com. Accessed February 5, 2021. goodreads.com/author/quotes/9810 .Albert_Einstein.

———. "Helen Keller Quotes." Goodreads.com. Accessed April 8, 2021. goodreads.com/author/quotes/7275.Helen_Keller.

———. "Michael Jordan Quotes " Goodreads.com. Accessed April 8, 2021. goodreads.com/quotes/10870-i-can-accept-failure -everyone-fails-at-something-but-i.

Haskins, Henry Stanley. *Meditations in Wall Street.* W. Morrow and Co., 1940.

Manning, Chelsea. "I Am a Transgender Woman and the Government Is Denying My Civil Rights." *Guardian*, December 8, 2014. theguardian.com/commentisfree/2014/dec/08/chelsea-manning -transgender-rights.

Mohr, Tara. "Playing Big Is Being More Loyal to Your Dreams Than to Your Fears." TaraMohr.com. Accessed April 22, 2021. taramohr.com.

Oprah.com. "What Oprah Knows for Sure about Finding the Courage to Follow Your Dreams." Accessed April 21, 2021. oprah.com/spirit /what-oprah-knows-for-sure-about-finding-your-dreams.

Quotefancy. "Discipline Is Built by . . ." Accessed April 8, 2021. quotefancy.com/quote/953308/Robin-S-Sharma-Discipline-is -built-by-consistently-performing-small-acts-of-courage.

———. "Never Give Up on a Dream Just Because of the Time . . ." Quotefancy.com. Accessed February 20, 2021. quotefancy.com /quote/31923.

Restauri, Denise. "This College Student Tracks Your Body as You Workout and Lose Weight." *Forbes*, December 9, 2013. forbes.com/sites/deniserestauri/2013/12/09/this-college -student-tracks-your-body-as-you-workout-and-lose-weight /?sh=315619dd5679.

Rosten, Leo. "On Finding Truth: Abandon the Strait Jacket of Conformity." Washington, DC, *Sunday Star*, April 8, 1962.

Sherman, James R. *Rejection.* Pathway Books, 1982.

Shriver, Maria. "Is It Time for a Reset?" MariaShriver.com. Accessed April 22, 2021. mariashriver.com/is-it-time-for-a-reset/.

Silicon Review. "'If Your Dreams Don't Scare You They Are Small' Says Richard Branson, Co-founder of Virgin Group," SiliconReview.com, June 1, 2018. thesiliconreview.com/2018/06/if-your -dreams-dont-scare-you-they-are-small-says-richard -branson-co-founder-of-virgin-group.

Steinem, Gloria. *My Life on the Road.* Random House, 2015.

Van Gogh, Vincent. Letter to Theo van Gogh, October 22, 1882. VanGoghLetters.org. vangoghletters.org/vg/letters/let274 /letter.html.

ACKNOWLEDGMENTS

I would like to acknowledge my teachers, clients, soul family, and team members of the past, present, and future who have contributed to my journey and who themselves have been catalysts for change within me. I would also love to acknowledge all the women whose shoulders I stand upon, who have risked so much to blaze the trail that I am now able to walk, both in the writing of this journal and in the broader scope of my work in the world. To all the devoted dreamers, change-makers, and visionaries blazing new trails for future generations who inspire me, and to each of you who have had a hand in making this possible, I am deeply grateful.

ABOUT THE AUTHOR

Emily Cassel is a Soulful Business + Leadership Coach for women entrepreneurs, podcast host, international retreat leader, champion of women, and believer that your big crazy dream is 100 percent possible.

With a background in positive psychology, sustainability, and spirituality, Emily is devoted to helping people launch, grow, and scale the business their soul came here to create, all while making the impact and income that changes their—and our—world.

Emily is driven by the belief that when a woman embraces and expresses her deepest soul calling, becomes a leader of her life and business, and does it in a way that's sustainable, she creates a more harmonious future for herself, the people around her, and our world. Emily gathers and grows both aspiring and established women entrepreneurs through her signature coaching experiences.

She is the creator of the Soulful Business Academy, the Business Alchemy Circle, and the Soulful Leadership Mastermind.

You can learn more about Emily's work and receive free support tools, resources, and trainings at EmilyCassel.com.